HOW TO...
BUILD it

HOW TO...
BUILD it

GROW YOUR BRAND

NIRAN VINOD & DAMOLA TIMEYIN

1 3 5 7 9 10 8 6 4 2

#Merky Books
20 Vauxhall Bridge Road
London SW1V 2SA

#Merky Books is part of the Penguin Random House group
of companies whose addresses can be found at global.
penguinrandomhouse.com.

Copyright © Niran Vinod, Damola Timeyin 2020

Niran Vinod and Damola Timeyin have asserted their right to be identified as the
authors of this Work in accordance with the Copyright, Designs and Patents Act 1988.

First published in the United Kingdom by #Merky Books in 2020

www.penguin.co.uk

A CIP catalogue record for this book is available from the British Library.

ISBN 9781529118803

Text Design © Andreas Brooks
Typeset in 10/13 pt Source Serif Variable Roman by Jouve (UK), Milton Keynes
Printed and bound in Great Britain by Clays Ltd, Elcograf, S.p.A.

Penguin Random House is committed to a sustainable future for our
business, our readers and our planet. This book is made from
Forest Stewardship Council® certified paper.

CONTENTS

FOREWORD BY NANDO'S

A lot of people have asked us over the years what the recipe for a successful brand is. But that's a bit like asking the recipe for PERi-PERi itself. It's a secret. Not just because we like to keep it quiet, but because a truly successful recipe is individual to a specific chef and their specific ingredients.

There's no one recipe for a great brand, but there are items that we believe every aspiring entrepreneur needs in the bag: a unique product, a place for your brand to live and its customers to thrive, the right people around you, and passion. Though, of course, each person will have their own signature flavours to add. But these four things – product, place, people, passion – are must-haves.

We knew we had the perfect ingredients for success back in 1987 when the idea for Nando's was sparked at a chicken grill in Jo'burg, South Africa. We were two determined, hardworking mates (soon to be business partners), at a cool place to eat (place), feasting on a tasty plate of chicken with Portuguese flavour and African fire (a unique product). These were the blocks we built our brand on, and it was our passion that pushed us all the way.

It hasn't all been plain sailing. Like any entrepreneurs we've made a few wrong decisions at times – but it's how you handle your mistakes that matter. Believe it or not, our first three sites didn't make much money when we first opened in London, but we hung in there. We knew we had something special, so we made each plate sold count. We also opened a Nando's in Ibiza many moons ago (we like to party) but we didn't foresee the quiet winters, so we – sadly – had to close. We've always turned our losses into lessons, through perseverance and knowing when to let go. Everyone fails at some point, but fail well and you'll never regret a mistake in your life.

Our food brings the unique spirit of Southern Africa to the world with our magic chillies, in a way that no one else can. Literally. Our African bird's eye chillies – the key to our legendary PERi-PERi sauce – are farmed sustainably under the Southern African sun exclusively for Nando's. That's what makes our product so special. Give your customers a unique product they can't get elsewhere, something to keep coming back for. That's what we did, and we now feed customers in almost every continent in the world.

Nando's might have been born out of South Africa, but it was made famous in the UK. We launched here in 1992 and grew our name with our fun, vibrant restaurants covered in original South African art. Our cosy-but-lively restaurants are designed to feel like a home away from home. But each is a gallery too, a place for you to feast your eyes, as well as to feast on our food. Creating special experiences like this beyond the product for your audience is vital; every successful brand has a visual hub.

We're now a proud staple of British culture, up there with Burberry and a cup of tea (at least, that's what we're told). Supporting local communities, creative industries and youth projects keeps us at the forefront of culture, and allows us to have fun with the brand whilst making a difference. We're truly a global brand in a digital age, connecting and collaborating with other inspirational people both offline and online, in our mission to help change lives.

You might not know this, but Nando's was founded on the principles of the Spirit of the Rainbow Nation: a post-apartheid South Africa where democracy, inclusivity and equality were champion. We launched at a time when divisions were high in South Africa, as they so often are throughout the world today. And we believe the spirit of the Rainbow Nation that drives us here at Nando's resonates today more than ever.

Every brand is more than just its product, and Nando's is more than just PERi-PERi and chips. We're founded on the empowerment of the people we serve, and employ to serve. Hiring good, passionate people and sticking by our values have been the key to our success.

The strongest brands today are those that make a lasting positive impact and have a meaningful relationship with their consumers. Put simply, they have a mission to do more. Good business makes more than just profit; it makes a better world. Our brand purpose, our 'why' is *'Changing Lives, Together'*. We wonder what purpose you will find to make this planet we share a better place to live? We're excited to find out.

Nando's is all about bringing people together. It's our ambition to fire up young people around the world; feeding more than just your appetites, but your imaginations too. That's why we're so happy to introduce this book brought to you by #Merky Books – an imprint whose dedication to bringing people together around the joy of reading, unlocking their creativity and investing in community we could not champion enough.

If we could let you young firestarters know one thing about building a brand it would be this: expect to get your hands dirty. Our success wasn't handed to us on a plate. We were the ones handing out the plates, around the clock. Tenacity and passion trump expertise and money any day. We didn't have business degrees or know about the restaurant industry when we started – but we were prepared to work hard and learn on the job. We put our minds to it even when others were doubtful. If we succeeded, so can you.

And lastly – don't forget to have fun! (Not too much though – if there's one thing Nando's Ibiza taught us it's *everything in moderation*.)

So, devour this book like you would any plate from Nando's. It's written by some of the UK's most exciting creative talent for you to learn from. We can't wait to see what big ideas you make happen with their advice!

Nando's,
2020

iNTRODUCTiON

SO YOU WANT TO BUILD A BRAND?

This may be the most challenging thing you ever decide to do. There will be tears, late nights, and moments when you wonder why you started in the first place. But we promise you, afterwards you'll look at what you've created and celebrate both the wins and the losses.

Building something that started as an idea in your mind and seeing it manifest in the real world is one of the most rewarding things you can do. You have the potential to influence lives, change culture and even make a bit of money along the way. All you have to do is start the journey. This book is your guide.

WHAT IS A BRAND ANYWAY?

A brand is the way a company, organisation or an individual is perceived by those who experience it. It's more than just the name, typeface or logo: it is how a product, business or campaign resonates with the customer. Brands are more than a superficial veneer around a business. Think of it as an invisible layer, wrapped around a product or service making it mean more in the mind of the customer.

As the term 'brand' can refer to either a company or an individual, we'll be looking at both – mainly how you can build your company's brand, as you set up and grow your business, but also how you can build your personal brand as you navigate through your career.

WHO ARE WE?

Between us we have spent twenty years working for some of the world's best agencies, on accounts for some of the world's biggest companies, and we have even built our own brands too.

Damola's experience building brands began during secondary school, in Year 10, with an entertainment brand called TimSon Productions that he created with a friend. They produced sold-out talent shows, long before Simon Cowell reinvigorated the format, and used the proceeds to pay for a month-long expedition to Ecuador.

Fast forward a few years, and, after a brief stint as a banker, Damola got the chance to help build brands professionally and learn from some of the brightest and best, at Dare (*Campaign's* 'Digital Agency of the Decade'), then at the renowned creative agency Bartle Bogle Hegarty and most recently at Facebook. In these places he developed social, digital and brand strategies for household names, among them Tesco, Virgin Media and Barclays Bank.

However, Damola's most enjoyable experiences have been when building his own brand, The Capture Collective, and helping to build and advise start-up brands, such as the bank for young people, Osper, the creative network, People of Culture Collective (PoCC), and, most recently, premium African vodka brand, Vusa. With each he got the opportunity to 'see under the hood', helping to make crucial decisions about the DNA of these brands and seeing the impact of these decisions in real life.

Niran's creative journey, meanwhile, began as a two-year-old, when his parents gave him his first set of LEGO, which allowed him to explore his imagination and build whatever came to mind. That feeling of building something from concept to execution is still what brings him the most joy, and is how he ended up learning design through magazine tutorials and forums at the age of thirteen, which then led to art school, to study creative advertising strategy.

Niran's time at art school exposed him to an environment he'd not come across before, one that expanded his horizons, and allowed him to create his own brand – a website, Yin&Yang, which grew organically and paved his route into the industry through an internship at WeAreSocial. There, he learned more in the two-month summer break than he had during his entire time at university, and, as a result, he was headhunted to work on the ASOS account at a small creative agency called Independents United (IU-HQ). After a few years, Niran then moved to one of the most innovative digital agencies in the world, AKQA, to work for his childhood dream client, Nike. He pivoted out of agency life in 2015, in order to move to Instagram as a Creative Strategist on the advertising side of the business, helping clients within the fashion e-commerce and luxury market. But, outside of his nine-to-five, he's always had side projects that fuel his creativity, from photography to art direction, and consulting on various brands' digital strategies.

HOW WE MET

We connected a decade ago on Twitter – off the back of a photography project that involved Niran capturing a photograph of London a day for a year.

A mutual follow based on both of us working in the same industry led to Damola reaching out a little while later to get Niran's thoughts on The Capture Collective, as he was in the process of setting it up. Then came the usual thing of bumping into each other at a plethora of music and industry events across the city, and we became friends, collaborators, colleagues and now co-authors.

WHY ARE WE WRITING THIS BOOK?

When we reflect on the brands and businesses we've attempted to build ourselves, it's hard not to shake our heads with a touch of regret. While valiant, our efforts sometimes didn't amount to much more than a couple of lines on a CV and stories to tell in a book.

However, we were both navigating the system without a metaphorical map, torchlights or a guide. As the children of first-generation immigrants, who had worked hard to create a good life for their families in the UK, our parents' objective had been for us to build on their success, which, as many will recognise, mainly meant: nail your education and settle into a stable, traditional job.

While we largely followed this pre-ordained path, there were lots of occasions where we'd intuitively try to navigate the system in a different way to what our families had envisaged – whether that was setting up a production company with a friend at school or a lifestyle brand after university. But we mainly used these 'side hustles' to demonstrate to potential employers that we had what it took to be a top-tier employee, instead of continuing to build these brands into something that could last. Yet, in hindsight, none of them actually had to be deviations off the main path. They could have *been* the path.

This is why we believe it's about time that advice normally reserved for the meeting rooms of advertising agencies and marketing departments is decoded and made available to people who wouldn't otherwise have access to these places or that information. This book is not a brand-building bible, as there are more qualified people out there writing those; it is a well-informed point of view on some of the things we wish we'd known when we started out. And if it helps one person navigate the system effectively or build a brand that becomes successful, writing this book will have been worth it.

WHAT ARE YOU GOING TO FIND BETWEEN THESE COVERS?

This book is for people who are building a brand for the first time. We'll set the scene with some tips on how to start your brand-building journey, then help you lay the foundations for your brand, and give you some ideas about how you share your brand with the world, followed by some nuggets that may be useful as you reflect on the journey you've been on.

STARTING THE JOURNEY

CHAPTER I

USE THE POWER OF YOUR NETWORK

While the responsibility for your brand or business begins and ends with you, it's unlikely that you will make it the success it should be alone. Building a brand starts with the people close to you, those who you trust to share your vision, and who can help you scale and build.

Damola's mum would often say to him: 'Show me your friends and I'll tell you who you are.' At times, these words felt like a warning, thinly disguised as loving advice. In hindsight, they bear more significance that he cared to realise and have helped guide him through his career.

So, if we want to build brands that last, we have to reflect on the people we surround ourselves with and consider who we want by our side on our journey. From close friendship groups to mentors and investors, having the right team around you at every stage of your brand-building journey will both prepare you for success and also help manage your missteps along the way.

IRON SHARPENS IRON

The expression 'iron sharpens iron' is another term Damola grew up hearing. He was sure it was an old Nigerian saying, but, no, it's a proverb from the

Bible that refers to iron blades being used to sharpen other iron blades, until they became useful tools. In your own context, having 'sharp' people around you can make you more effective at what you do.

So, as you build your brand, don't be afraid of *not* being the smartest person in the room. If you *are* the smartest person in the room, then, frankly, you need to find another room. Make it your mission early on to find your 'iron' – that person who is sharper than you and can push your thinking. Proximity to that person, whether in a physical space, or virtually, will inevitably sharpen your ideas as well as your output.

Let's look at pop culture for a second and see this principle in action. Take the life of American artist Jean-Michel Basquiat – the rapper Jay-Z's favourite artist – who, by the time of his death, had risen from street graffiti artist to legendary neo-expressionist painter. Basquiat emerged in the context of 1970s New York, a period of political and economic turmoil, where emerging creatives found the early rap, punk and street-art scenes coalescing. This environment brought him and other notable pop art artists, such as Keith Haring, Kenny Scharf, Fab 5 Freddy and, later, Andy Warhol, together.

WHERE CAN YOU FIND LIKE-MINDED PEOPLE TO SHARPEN YOUR SKILLS?

1. **TWITTER COMMUNITIES** – Your network on Twitter will inevitably revolve around your interests as well as your friends. When they collide, friends can become collaborators.

2. **LINKEDIN COMMUNITIES** – LinkedIn is a useful place to find people with similar professional interests. It allows you to connect with experts from around the world and participate in conversations as if you were in a classroom or lecture hall.

3. **UNIVERSITY ALUMNI COMMUNITIES** – Many universities create alumni groups, which are full of people who have gone on to do a range of different things. You'll be surprised by the amount of experience only an email away.

While Basquiat's innate talent was unquestionable, being connected to a community of progressive artists had an undeniable influence and impact on his art, which would later be regarded as ground-breaking.

The Warhol to your Basquiat could be within arms' reach. Plug into your local or industry-based networks and connect with people who are willing to share their passion, expertise and experience with you.

YOU NEED MORE THAN YOUR 'DAY ONES' TO SUCCEED

Our favourite Canadian rapper, Drake, made the 'No New Friends' motto famous, with the song of the same name, but his own entourage is proof that you need your 'Day Ones', those who've been there from the beginning (i.e. Day One), as well as your 'Day 100s' to build successfully.

Both of us have been there for friends. We've been the 'Day Ones', helping them launch start-ups, but we've also been the 'Day 100s', the experts helping a brand grow.

As you build your brand, you'll need a whole squad of different people to help:

THE DOERS – Those who will stop at nothing till the job is done

THE RIDE OR DIES – Those who look risk in the eye and tell it to 'do one'

THE GENERALISTS – Those who are happy to turn their hand to most things, as there will be lots to do

THE SPECIALISTS – Those who know a lot about a specific thing and can help you grow in a very specific way

THE EXPERIENCED – Those who will use their experience and expertise to lead aspects of the brand or business in your absence, because you can't do everything

Are you going to be great at everything? That's unlikely. You will go further by focusing on your strengths, understanding your weaknesses and assembling a team of people that complement each other, than you will trying to be a one-person band.

As you assemble the crew that will help you build this brand – make it diverse, make it inclusive, make it intersectional. It's proven that diverse and inclusive teams lead to better results.

As two men writing a book, we understand that our voice is typically the loudest. However, we build and grow brands at work with an exceptionally talented, inclusive team around us that make it happen because of the nuances and different perspectives they bring to the table.

Diversity and inclusion isn't a fad. We're not advising you to do this because diversity and inclusion are the idea du jour, we're recommending this because it's a game-changing strategy that makes a difference. Especially if everyone who has a seat at the table also has a voice at that table.

SOMEONE HAS TO TELL YOU THE TRUTH

Accountability is not about someone telling you what to do, or about being chastised when things go wrong; accountability is a tool that ensures you reach your potential. Most businesses have this, in the shape of a board of directors whose purpose is to make sure the company is moving in the right direction, and who represent the interests of key shareholders and stakeholders. If a business has a board of directors, why shouldn't you?

A great tool for ensuring accountability is having a 'personal board of directors', who are different to the people helping you do the day to day. These people are different to the 'team' listed above: they should offer a different perspective, some home truths, and guidance – another layer of accountability to ensure you reach your vision.

Creating your own personal board of directors can be an informal process. You certainly don't need to hold interviews, and your 'directors' shouldn't need a salary.

In most cases, you may already have these people around you, but not know it. And, if not, reach out. On your personal board you should have someone who:

- **CAN CRITIQUE YOU** – They will give you honest and sensible advice without you catching feelings

- **YOU ASPIRE TO BE** – A person with the type of skills and experience that you want to have yourself in the future

- **HAS SIMILAR EXPERIENCE TO YOU** – Someone who understands your perspective and experience and can put themselves in your shoes

- **IS FROM A DIFFERENT GENERATION** – This person brings the benefit of age, and sees life through a different lens

Treat this seriously. Extend an invitation and approach people with a personal touch. Explain your rationale for approaching them specifically, your goals, and, if they're up for it, agree to a way of working together that suits both of you.

IRL TO URL

With the emergence of the internet and online social platforms, we all went from a place of being connected to a small set of friends and family to a wider globally-connected network of friends and acquaintances. The ability to connect and reach out to anyone, find answers to any question, learn anything and everything, has significantly changed our culture. The democratisation of technology has fuelled economic transformation, creativity and the birth of many new sectors and jobs, including our own, which wouldn't have existed twenty years ago.

Niran in particular wouldn't be where he is in both his life and his work without the internet. As with so many people, it has played a huge part in his personal relationships for a start. Pre-app-based dating, he met his now wife through a random tweet that sparked their initial conversation, and (many years later) they're still together and have a child. The internet massively assisted his career too: expanding his skill set and creating a wider network of peers and acquaintances across the globe. It may make us sound old, but everything seemed to evolve organically in the early days of the internet. There was a natural evolution, rather than the constant imperative to always be connected that we have today. Your relationships transitioned through close friendship circles, to forums, to meet-ups. Now, connectedness is mandated by convenience – at the tip of our fingers, bringing us ever closer to our network.

URL TO IRL

In the beginning, URL life was hard – you had to be patient in order to even get online. Niran vividly remembers the day the internet connection was set up at his parents' house, back in 1998. The mechanical 56k dial-up tone would make high-pitched sounds whenever it was disconnected or, more frequently in Niran's case, whenever someone called on the landline. But the connection was sufficient for him to start checking out Photoshop tutorials and joining relevant forums that interested him. Back then it was all football related or, better yet, football-design related.

Forums were akin to what creative WhatsApp groups are now – a closed group of peers. We made friends and would continue conversations through MSN. We masked ourselves behind avatars and began all interactions with three simple letters – A/S/L (i.e. Age/Sex/Location). Fast-forward fifteen years and strangers follow and comment on your posts – you return the follow, eventually end up in a conversation, and go on to meeting up IRL and becoming friends. This can happen for both personal and professional relationships, and may end up significantly changing one's life and career opportunities.

EXPANDING YOUR SKILLSET

Much of Niran's early design craft was learnt without having any formal education.

The internet is a free gateway to endless possibilities in terms of expanding your repertoire of skills or knowledge. We live in an open-source economy: there is a democracy of information exchange through multiple official platforms, such as Skillshare, MasterClass, Lynda.com, and even YouTube tutorials, from a horde of different kinds of people – chefs, carpenters, 3D designers – sharing knowledge/skills, all of which can empower you and develop your skillset arsenal.

WHERE TO START LEARNING ONLINE

Niran has thoroughly enjoyed subscribing to MasterClass during the Covid-19 lockdown and bingeing on the knowledge being passed on from people who have 'made it', such as Bob Iger, Steph Curry and Sara Blakely.

Niran highly recommends his friend Sophia Chang's Skillshare classes on how to build your digital presence and optics in the digital age.

YouTube is a great place to start as it is free. Pick a topic that you'd like to learn; anything from video editing to creating a website.

SHOW, DON'T TELL

It's all too easy to claim you can do x and y in your social media bio or LinkedIn profile but, when it comes down to it, actually demonstrating your ability to do your craft, and do it well, does all the talking for you.

When Niran was studying at the London College of Communication, he and a classmate became frustrated by endless lectures that repeated out-of-date information, or information that had no viable connection to what they were seeing every day. This was in the very early days of the rise of social media platforms, with the resultant proliferation of blogs and websites. Niran and his friend saw a gap and started their own: Yin&Yang. Without any prior knowledge, strategy or thought to the word 'influencers', they bought a domain name and started to post their opinions on fashion, street culture, music and art in London. It was all intuitive, capturing the essence of their London as they experienced it, as young twenty-year-olds who were trying to make something of themselves.

The website quickly transitioned into a platform for them to create original content for brands, centred around their audience's interests. They learnt how by reading up and doing, often working with mediums new to them, such as photography and videography, to communicate their vision.

The on-the-go experience added a new layer to Niran's CV, on which he could confidently include – and then, more importantly, show – his individual way of doing things. Beyond the creative output side of building a website, Yin&Yang also got both Niran and his friend out of the comfort zone of university life. Between lectures, they took meetings with agencies and brands who trusted them to feature their product launches and upcoming collaborations. Sitting across the table from brand managers and PR execs in order to negotiate and pitch was not exactly part of their lesson plan. But, as a result, they were able to develop their 'soft' skills. If 'hard' skills are what you require to get things done – for example, if you're an engineer, your programming and coding knowledge are your 'hard' skills – 'soft' skills are what you require to interact with others and express yourself. They are much harder to measure.

ADDING TO YOUR CONTACTS

The internet eliminates certain boundaries to access. However, the ability to reach out to a stranger you respect and only know digitally still requires skill and sincerity.

TIP

List your projects and experiences outside of your nine-to-five and education. For Niran, listing Yin&Yang on his CV showcased his entrepreneurial spirit, diversity of experience and drive to create something that was his own, outside of his day job.

We both get people diving into our inboxes and DMs with messages asking us to meet up for a coffee, or for a job referral to our respective companies. That's not the right approach when asking for an introduction, or when meeting with a possible mentor.

Ways to ask:

— Be human and sincere.

— Be clear on your ask. Don't overdo it with an essay that puts off the receiver from understanding what you're after.

— Sign off sincerely. Niran has used the following template for any emails like this for the past decade:

I understand if you're too busy to answer in detail or don't have the time to respond at the moment. However, if have any advice or thoughts, they would be greatly appreciated.

Thanks in advance.

NETWORK = NET WORTH

The term 'networking' has become tainted as a result of too many corporate events that involve too much small talk, with forced interactions over small bites and craft beer, and that ever-present question – 'what do you do?' A simple question with big punch. When building Yin&Yang, Niran and his co-founder immersed themselves in environments where the conversation was easy, skill sharing was all around, and their 'tribe' evident, as was what they wanted to share/profile with the world.

In real life, after you say hello, and before you jump to what it is you 'do', you can instead create a much more enjoyable conversation around your interests and passion projects, rather than focusing on hierarchies and clout.

The new ways of networking are:

— Sharing/reposting work you admire (comment, share and engage in conversation with those you admire)

— Sharing stories (e.g. over a coffee, tea, walk)

— Sharing projects together (create something)

— Sharing success (bring someone else in if a job is not right for you)

INTROVERTS AND EXTROVERTS

Niran considers himself an introvert. He's not the loudest voice in the room, and not one to willingly stand in a room full of strangers. He used to think that put him at a disadvantage, but remember: it's just as much about the work you do as what you say, so you can let it speak for you. This is something that Niran learned quickly in the early days of the website, and it has been reinforced again and again throughout his career.

There will be a time when you will need to advocate for yourself and your brand, however – how to do that in a way you're comfortable with is key.

Damola is slightly different to Niran, in that he feels he sits between being an introvert and an extrovert. He gets his energy from being around other people and, unlike Niran, he likes standing up in front of people and presenting. Despite this, in a meeting, Damola can take a step back, listen and understand other people's perspective before sharing his own. Being able to flex between the two types of personality is something that he's actively developed over the years and will apply depending on the time and place.

So, in conclusion, always:

— Meet on solid ground – where is comfortable for you? Make an effort to meet where it's easier for them.

— Be honest – be genuine and interested in someone's work, and respectful of their time.

— Say hello 'just because' from time to time – don't just reach out when you need something.

— Send thanks – following up is just as important as reaching out.

CHAPTER 2

GET YOUR MIND RIGHT

COMPARISON IS THE DEATH OF JOY

We're living in an age where so many distractions exist in the palm of our hand. It's far too easy to pick up your phone and aimlessly scroll through social media feeds, not getting anything done. Faced with what your peers are doing with their brands or how they're levelling up with new career moves, it's hard not to start comparing your own achievements and progress (or the lack thereof). While it is important to know the market and what your competitors are doing for strategic planning, focusing too heavily on others can be detrimental to your own output.

Here are a few tips to break the ol' habit of comparison:

— Count your blessings. Look at what you have, rather than what you haven't got yet.

— Imperfection is fine. Perfection can stifle creativity. Learn from the process.

— Comparison with others isn't a fair way to measure progress: instead look at your own journey over the last few weeks, months and years to where you are now.

It's easy to beat yourself up while comparing yourself to others, but remember that your journey is unique. So trust and enjoy the process – the ups *and* the downs.

SACRIFICE FOR SUCCESS

When Niran was running Yin&Yang, it was always outside of his day job and took up much of his evenings and weekends – from managing emails and potential client meetings during lunch hours to evening meetings planning projects with the team. For many of our peers, these were prime socialising times, but he knew he had to make sacrifices if he wanted to take the website to the next level. Make every day count by setting specific goals and creating patterns in your life, in order to energise your brand and sustain it. Sacrifices will be necessary at different stages along the journey, but make sure you maintain a healthy balance – especially for your mental wellbeing. Here's a few tips that Niran has learnt over the past ten-plus years of working.

— Find a routine that works for you. It takes time but some people are morning people and others are night owls – finding a work schedule that caters to you is essential.

— Rest and recovery are important. Just like fitness training, being well rested is just as important for your creativity and productivity.

- The power of no. Saying 'no' more often to ensure that you don't spread yourself too thin does yourself and your brand justice.

- Mindfulness and meditation. There's a plethora of online apps and programs like Calm and Headspace that can take you through a daily guided meditation practice to help centre yourself and be present.

TURNING VISION INTO REALITY WITH OBJECTIVES

WHY OBJECTIVES ARE IMPORTANT

If, like us, you're someone who always has a million different creative ideas flying around in their head, it's quite easy to just keep them floating there and not see them through. Ideas are cheap – execution is key. Clear goal-setting will provide structure and clarity for you, your team and your brand. (We find writing your objectives down physically really useful, as they act as a constant reminder.)

Before Niran got his job at Instagram, he wrote down exactly what he wanted from his next role, and stuck it up on his wall as a daily reminder of what he was after, and to help filter out opportunities that wouldn't help him get there.

SMART

We all tend to generalise our goals when we start out, and they're usually too broad: things like 'get new business'. But *how many* customers? Is there a deadline? Revise your goals to something more achievable and specific, such as 'Get two new business clients by the end of next month'. This is what we call a SMART goal.

SMART objectives are a great tool to use when setting personal or business brand goals. SMART stands for:

SPECIFIC – Adapt the goal so it is specific to your brand or your personal needs.

MEASURABLE – Make your goals quantifiable. Having a measurable goal helps you identify when the target has been reached.

ACHIEVABLE – Set a target that's right in terms of achievability. It needs to be not so hard it'll make you stress and become discouraged when (inevitably) you don't get there, but not so easy that it doesn't lead to any growth.

REALISTIC – Set objectives that you can achieve in the near term and build from there. No big brand is built overnight. The difference between realistic and achievable is the former focuses more on what is deliverable in the near term, based on the current climate and the resources that you have.

TIME-BOUND – Deadlines are crucial. Niran is the type of person who'll procrastinate as much as possible till crunch time and the pressure fuels him to 'get in the zone'.

Ultimately, clear-cut objectives are a great way to bring your vision to reality, and will act as a reminder and a tracker of progress along the journey.

EXERCISE: If you've started building your brand, what are the objectives you've set yourself?

Use this exercise to turn them into SMART objectives.

....

....

....

....

....

CHAPTER 3

BUILD
TO
LEARN

10,000 HOURS AND CRAFT

Working on your craft over time is what makes you good – practice makes perfect, as the saying goes. Malcolm Gladwell famously introduced the 10,000-hours rule, in his book *Outliers*, as a way of achieving expertise in a skill. With a brand, that translates into diligently reiterating and tweaking your product and offering.

This brings us to a story about the late, great basketball player Kobe Bryant, who was known for his intense work ethic (which was dubbed the Mamba Mentality, as Bryant's nickname was 'the Black Mamba'). Former Chicago Bulls point guard Jay Williams recalls a regular season game against Bryant's team, the Los Angeles Lakers, where he decided to head to the court early ahead of the game to practise and was shocked to see Kobe there before him. Kobe was already sweating like crazy and stayed on even after Williams had left. The Mamba then proceeded to score forty points against Jay and the Bulls during the game itself. Jay approached him afterwards to ask why he'd trained for so long. Bryant replied: 'Because I saw you come in and I wanted you to know that it doesn't matter how hard you work – I am willing to work harder than you. You inspire me to be better.'

For us, that story sums up the importance of hunger and passion: talent by itself will only get you so far, to truly fly you'll need to graft.

MORE THAN JUST A NUMBERS GAME

Besides asking for the verified blue tick on Instagram, the second most common reason people get in touch with Niran has always been related to the Instagram feed algorithm and engagement issues. They're looking for tricks to hack profile growth numbers or, alternatively, to complain about lack of engagement. But creativity and craft should always supersede numbers and engagement metrics. At the end of the day, your business and craft is more than just a profile or page on a platform. You should aim to build a brand that is sustainable, beyond social clout and online hype; one built on credibility and longevity.

THE GROWTH MINDSET

'Growth' is a word you've probably heard bandied about a lot and you'll hear it a few times in this book.

Whether it's financial, market share or customer count, everyone's always chasing growth.

The term 'growth mindset' was coined by psychologist and author Carol Dweck. In her seminal book, *Mindset: The New Psychology of Success*, Dweck shows how success can be influenced by how we *think* about our abilities, and explores the two ways people can think about ability:

— Growth mindset: the belief that abilities can be developed, regardless of where your starting point is.

— Fixed mindset: the belief that abilities are fixed and cannot be developed.

We believe that, if you're embarking on the process of building a brand, the belief that you and your team have the potential to develop is crucial.

Those with a growth mindset will actively seek new knowledge, whether through books, other people or observation of what others have built. Meanwhile, someone with a fixed mindset is likely to stick to their limited supply of information, knowledge and experience, resulting in stagnation and repeated mistakes.

As you build your brand, make personal learning a habit. At the end of every quarter, write down what you've learnt about the brand-building process and what you've learnt personally, and identify what you want to learn in the next quarter. Seek out relevant sources of information as you reach new milestones and discover new needs.

EXERCISE:

What have you learnt in the last three months about building your brand?

....

....

What do you want to learn in the next three months about building your brand?

....

....

What are you going to do differently based on what you've learnt?

....

....

SETTING THE FOUNDATIONS

CHAPTER 4

EVERY BRAND NEEDS A STORY

KNOWING YOUR POINT OF DIFFERENCE

Ultimately, your story is unique to you – your lived experience, your career achievements are all personal. Learning to speak your truth and communicate that in a succinct manner will be impactful and will enable people to understand what you have to offer.

You will have to do this when hiring your personal board of directors or when you tell people in passing what you do. Communicating your brand's point of difference is the next level up and will prepare you for communicating your brand purpose and proposition en masse.

We'll come back to brand purpose and brand proposition, but, for now, think of them as:

BRAND PURPOSE – The reason why your brand does what it does.

BRAND PROPOSITION – What your brand promises to do for the consumer.

Niran's first experience of knowing his own point of difference was when he was asked to go back to his alma mater, LCC (London College of Communication), and share his career journey to a room full of final-year students. He already knew how to convey his personal story in the context of job interviews – mentioning past endeavours and his work/portfolio to date – but this was something else. If an interview was going well, it would tip into the informal, feeling fluid; when delivering a talk, or making a pitch, you need a clear flow and narrative.

With a simple opening slide, and a short sentence, where he landed was this:

> 'My truth. Niran Vinod, Brown Guy, Londoner, Creative Strategist, ~~Photographer, Creative Director,~~ Gamer, Vigilante. I just like making stuff.'

Firstly, it was personal – Niran has always embraced the most obvious parts of who he is. And it was a good icebreaker – it helped his nerves, and got the audience to loosen up by adding in a bit of humour. But, most importantly, it was a short and simple – allowing him to then go on to expand on each word, and share his story in depth. Yet it also showed his growth – crossing out his past endeavours was a way of showing how he got to where he is now, and what he still likes doing. It also emphasises that a job title doesn't define who he is.

Building and presenting your personal brand requires you to truly know and understand your story, and be strategic in how you present and create a narrative that is true to your values. This leads onto your CV, which some may feel isn't as impactful in making a first impression as it is a very traditional form. However, your CV can be more than a Word document. It can be achieved in a number of creative ways. Perhaps the best way to present yourself is using a video, or making a poster, or is it something relevant to the person reading your application, and where you're applying? CVs can still be a great way to make a first impression.

TIP: HOW TO CONQUER YOUR CV

The same process of simplicity, and communicating your personal values, can be applied to your CV.

Here's what we look for:

— Personality. Too often we see a generic introduction paragraph filled with generic buzzwords; we want to know more about the person and why they think they're the right for the role.

— Keep it concise.

— List your notable achievements. Not everything has to be thrown in, just the impactful and defining moments of your journey.

HOW TO MAKE PEOPLE GIVE A SHIT

Everywhere you go, you'll find brands trying to communicate with you. How many of those brands have you noticed? And, of the ones you've noticed, how many do you genuinely care about? Be honest.

Because there are more important things in life, getting people to give a shit about brands is difficult, but it *is* possible.

To get people to genuinely buy into you and your brand, the layers beneath need to be good enough to care about. Otherwise the brand is just 'lipstick on a pig'.

Assuming what lies beneath the brand isn't a pig, in order to get people to care, a brand has to add value to consumers' lives and it can do this in different ways:

PROVIDE

SOCIAL VALUE Give them social currency	**MORAL VALUE** Back a cause that is relevant to them
EMOTIONAL VALUE Make them love, laugh, cry etc	**FUNCTIONAL VALUE** Solve a problem or do something useful

Doing these things isn't enough, however: a brand also has to find a way of connecting with consumers and making them realise what the brand offers is something they *need* in their lives.

Getting people to care, as we said, is difficult. Your job is to use creativity to persuade them, finding ways to be relevant to their lives and selling your brand with clarity and simplicity.

Back in 2010, when Damola was still working as a banker, he had a desperate need for a creative outlet in his life. He'd done creative things that had brought him enjoyment in the past, but he wanted to learn something new, so he picked up photography. At the same time, he decided he wanted to create a brand that helped new photographers, such as he was, capture and showcase their photographs in real life, not just on the 'gram, and so The Capture Collective was born.

Damola thought the idea was cool and, in his mind, he knew what the brand was, but when he told people about it, it was clear no one else shared his enthusiasm or understood what he was aiming for. He needed to get people to care the same way he did about this thing he was trying to build. Many years later, once he got his story straight, he was vindicated, and managed to grow both The Capture Collective brand and community, but, until he did, progress was slow.

The experience taught him an important lesson and gave him a great exercise to use when working with brands, which you can use too:

EXERCISE: Why should people care about your brand? List three reasons why your target audience should care about your brand:

1

....

....

....

2

....

....

....

3

....

....

....

If you want people to care, you need to get your story straight. Your story gives your brand meaning, helps consumers understand the brand and the value it can add to their lives.

Many people have built successful brands without having gone through the process of getting their brand's story straight, especially at the beginning, but if you take the time now to figure this stuff out, it will clear a lot of stuff up for you as you grow. It will also give you confidence when talking about your brand to other people and make them realise you understand what you're talking about, as well as giving you a sense of clarity about what your brand is all about and serve as the foundations that you can build your brand upon. Most importantly, defining your story will help you make solid decisions about what you should do and shouldn't do as your brand grows.

BUILDING YOUR BRAND STORY

The BBC show *Who Do You Think You Are?* selects famous people and traces their family history – discovering secrets and surprises at each turn. The end result is an emotional celebrity with a better sense of where they've come from, who they are, and what their purpose is in life. The process of building your brand story is not too dissimilar. By asking these questions about your brand, you get a better sense of what it is today, plus what it aspires to be in the future and why.

A big part of defining your brand story starts with that 'why', and asking yourself, 'Why does your brand exist in the first place?'

CRAFTING YOUR 'WHY'

In his now famous TED Talk, 'How Great Leaders Inspire Action', marketeer Simon Sinek said: 'People don't buy what you do, they buy why you do it.' What does he mean by that? He means that people sometimes care about *why* your brand exists as well as *what* your brand sells. That 'why' is what is known as a brand's purpose: its reason for existing.

Even some of the biggest brands in the world realise that they can't just sell to succeed. They need a purpose that goes beyond money and have built their businesses around this.

NIKE – To bring inspiration and innovation to every athlete* in the world. *If you have a body, you are an athlete.

TESLA – To accelerate the world's transition to sustainable energy.

INNOCENT – To make natural, delicious, healthy drinks that help people live well and die old.

FENTY BEAUTY – Beauty for all.

> *We both love the brand purpose of Fenty Beauty by Rihanna. It exemplifies how a great purpose defines all you do, and becomes a beacon that is impossible to ignore. In an official statement about her line of make-up, Rihanna said, 'Fenty Beauty was created for everyone: for women of all shades, personalities, attitudes, cultures, and races. I wanted everyone to feel included.' Rihanna is far from a silent partner in her brand. Everything about Fenty Beauty is aligned with what we know about her as an artist and advocate.*

TIP

Whether you're an industry insider or not, we're sure you could probably name a brand that's jumped on the 'purpose' train. There are certain brands out there ostentatiously displaying behaviour akin to Mother Teresa and then acting like comic book villains behind the scenes. It's generally easy to spot because it is so inauthentic. The PR disaster is inevitable, but it also serves as a lesson to anyone trying to define their purpose. Don't be too pious and try not to stray 'outside of your lane'. You're a brand, not a Byzantine monk.

WHEN DEFINING WHAT YOUR PURPOSE IS, ASK YOURSELF FOUR QUESTIONS:

— Is your 'why' relevant to your brand?

— Is your 'why' relevant to what's happening in the world today?

— Is your 'why' relevant to your audience?

— Is your 'why' solving a problem?

EXERCISE: What is your 'why'?

Think about why you set up your brand. What is its reason for being? How can it impact your community, the world around you or change a particular issue?

....

....

....

....

TIP

Why don't you complete this exercise with your personal board of directors?

All this work will ultimately lead to your brand vision . . .

CRAFTING YOUR 'WHERE'

Understanding 'why' your brand does what it does will help you define 'where' you want your brand to be in the future: your brand's vision.

The best time to think about where you want to be in the future is at the beginning. Why? As many of our creative friends tell us, 'The beginning of the creative process is where we feel like we have the most freedom. By the time you reach the end, the options no longer feel endless.'

So, if you're at the beginning of the brand-building process, this is your chance to feel the same freedom and be ambitious. Think about what your brand's vision should be. Think big in order to reach an end goal which doesn't feel limiting, rather limitless.

EXERCISE: Think big and be brave.

Where would you want to take your brand if there was no risk and you had £1,000,000?

....

....

What text message would you like to send your mum about your brand three years from now?

....

....

What headline would you like to see in *Forbes* magazine about your brand in the future?

....

....

WHY SHOULD YOU HAVE A BRAVE BRAND VISION?

— Stops you from aiming too low

— Gives you a 'north star' to aim for

— Sends a signal to others that you mean business

Great visions set the ambition for where the brand wants to be in the future, in a simple and tangible way. McDonalds' vision is a good example of this in action.

MCDONALDS – Our aim is to provide a fun and safe environment where our customers can enjoy good food made with quality ingredients at affordable prices.

EXERCISE: What is your vision for your brand?

....

....

....

....

....

....

....

....

....

....

Take a moment to review the vision you've written and ask yourself the following questions:

— Is it aspirational?

— Is it simple and specific?

— Is it relatable to your audience?

— Is it something that you would be proud of?

CRAFTING THE 'WHAT'

Now you've defined your 'why' and your 'where', think about 'what' your brand is selling and how you communicate that to people. In the marketing world we call this the brand's proposition.

Your audience should be in no doubt about 'what' your brand offers. If you can't articulate what you are selling, it will be difficult to persuade people to choose your brand over another one.

EXERCISE: In two sentences describe what you offer to your customer.

....

....

When describing what your brand does, it's common to overcomplicate it and forget that, above all, you are trying to persuade someone that what you do is worth paying for. There are five principles that we ask clients to consider when crafting their proposition:

1. Is it easy for people to understand?

2. Is it interesting enough for people to remember?

3. Does it explain how the brand is different?

4. Does it have clear benefit for the consumer?

5. Is it relevant to people's lives?

In the early days of building your brand, you may not be making TV advertisements that explain who you are and what you do, but you will still want to tell people what your brand is all about. Crafting a proposition means you have one or two sentences to hand that you can use, every time someone asks you about your brand.

Some of our favourite examples come from brands who do complicated things but have done a great job of making their proposition very simple.

UBER – We ignite opportunity by setting the world in motion.

SOUNDCLOUD – Find the music you love. Discover new tracks. Connect directly with your favourite artists.

PATCH PLANTS – We want to help bring the joy of gardening to anyone and everyone.

Another question we often ask clients is, 'How is your proposition different?' While it can be argued that imitation is the greatest form of flattery, there is no point building a brand that is exactly the same as something else that already exists. Your job is to find a way of making what you do different from what already exists and finding a way to make your brand look and feel different from other brands.

EXERCISE: How is your brand different?

....

....

....

....

....

Difference can come from lots of places:

— The product or service you offer

— The way your brand looks and feels

— The brand's 'tone of voice'

— The brand's behaviour

— Where it fits in the market

— You, the founder

As most things can be copied, the most powerful form of difference comes from having a differentiated 'product' or 'service'. If your product or service exists in the marketplace already, don't despair – you can use your brand to bring it to the market in a way that no one has tried before. It's not easy, but finding a new and different way to present your brand's proposition to the world can be done, and can set you apart in your category and beyond.

CHAPTER 5

WHAT ARE YOUR VALUES?

A brand's values guide what you do and don't do. Where you aim for, and where you settle. It even dictates what you look and sound like. Imagine your values as a bit like the angel on your shoulder that stops you doing something that you may regret later. This is exactly how your brand values play out as well, which we'll touch upon later.

GENERATIONAL LESSONS

Your brand's values are informed by who you are as a person first and foremost.

For Niran, it makes sense to take it back to his roots, as he did in his presentation to the students at LCC. He's the proud son of immigrants who came to England/London from India via Singapore in the 1970s. His parents worked in factories in the East End, so their own children could afford to go to university and get white-collar jobs. Niran's dad's favourite mantra was: 'I work hard so you and your sister can have a better life than me.' Growing up, Niran took those words on the chin, and didn't fully grasp what he was saying. It's only now, as a father himself, that he can fully relate to what his old man was saying. He now understands the sacrifices his father made as a parent, and that instilling a good work ethic starts young. Hard work and kindness were what his parents instilled in him from a young age, and as he's grown older and transitioned into a professional career, he's sought that in the projects he's created and in the brands he's worked for.

Niran realises it's a privilege that he's worked with companies that share his values of diversity, inclusivity and building social value within their company cultures.

BRANDS WITH STRONG ROOTS

Let's look at that global sportswear powerhouse, Nike. Their mantra is 'to bring inspiration and innovation to every athlete', and, as far as Nike are concerned, if you have a body, you *are* an athlete. Their roots are in performance and innovation, from their very first running spike, made by Bill Bowerman for Phil Knight, through to Tinker Hatfield-designed Air Jordans and to Virgil Abloh's recent take on the classic Waffle Racer. They've created products to enable people to excel at athletics and that remains true to this very day.

TIP

Louis Vuitton is arguably the world's most valuable luxury brand, and the reason for this is its strong brand identity, the brand DNA, which has been built carefully and gradually over the years. It has a cautious approach to brand extensions, for example, as well as a strict distribution strategy and a no-discount policy, all of which has helped preserve the brand's enviable profile and which harks back to its roots.

DEFINING YOUR VALUES

In order to figure out what the values of your brand are, start by going back to your roots and identifying what beliefs are important to you, and which of them you think are important and relevant to your brand.

EXERCISE: If your brand was a person, what would they believe in, what would they stand for, and how would they behave?

....

....

....

What do you do next with the answers to these questions? Filter them by deciding which of them:

— are aligned with your brand's purpose and vision

— are relevant today and are likely to be relevant in the future

— are realistic standards for your brand to live by

— are likely to trigger positive actions and behaviours internally

Damola went through this exercise with African vodka brand Vusa and creative network, People of Culture Creative (PoCC). Both brands came to him with an idea of their product, and their community, and it was Damola's job to help them create values that clearly articulated what the brand believed in, what it stood for and how it behaved.

VUSA BRAND VALUES

1. **PASSION** – We believe in passionately challenging cultural bias.

2. **EXUBERANCE** – We are a vodka with African energy.

3. **DISRUPTION** – We stand for changing the way people think about African craft and quality.

SINGING FROM THE SAME HYMN SHEET

Back in 2014, Damola was enjoying some time off before starting a new position at Bartle Bogle Hegarty, one of the best advertising agencies in the world. Their name and reputation preceded them: they'd made some of the most iconic adverts of all time and there was a certain aura around 60 Kingly Street, their head office.

A few weeks before his start date, he received an email from them. He initially assumed it was a generic email, but it turned out to be a personal

POCC BRAND VALUES

1. **PROGRESSIVE CREATIVITY** – We stand for taking original and non-traditional approaches to creating impactful creative work.

2. **OPENLY DIFFERENT** – We stand for being open about the authenticity and difference that powers everything we do.

3. **CULTURE OF GROWTH** – We stand for enhancing the personal and professional growth of our members.

4. **COMMUNITY RESPECT** – We stand for relationships that are respectful and believe our output should respect the communities that it portrays.

video welcoming him to the company. It went through the history of the business, the story of the founders and some of the company's core values: 'None of us are as good as all of us,' and, 'Advertising is 80 per cent idea, but it is also 80 per cent execution.'

These values remain as true today as when BBH was first established, over thirty years ago.

We believe that brand values are just as important for those who work for the brand as they are for the people buying your brand. Strong values shape brand culture and can influence your employee well-being. Create values that are fit for a diverse and inclusive organisation. At best, your values should inspire people to do the best work of their careers. At the very least, your values should make everyone feel welcome.

CHAPTER 6

KNOW YOUR AUDIENCE

You've done the work of finding out what your brand is about. Now it's time to think about how your brand exists in the real world. In the same way that culture doesn't happen in a vacuum, you can't build a brand without thinking about your audience. So ask yourself: 'Do you know who you're speaking to?'

EVERYONE IS NOT YOUR AUDIENCE

A lot of questions will play on a loop in your head at this point, as you reflect on your values, vision and proposition.

A big question will be: 'Who is this brand for and how do I connect with them?'

The trick here is being realistic, because as ambitious as it may be to want to appeal to *everyone* – you can't. Catering to *everyone* is dangerous.

Audiences are much more nuanced than you may realise (don't worry, we'll come back to this), and you can't please everyone all the time. You also don't have infinite resources in order to do so.

Being specific about who your audience is at the start means you will be able to address their particular needs well. And the unintended consequence of addressing a core audience's needs well is that *other* people may begin to recognise you for nailing it with *that* audience, and come to your brand as a result.

FINDING YOUR CORE AUDIENCE

In every city there is what we'll call a 'cultural Mecca'. When Damola was working in Soho in central London, even amidst the rampant gentrification, there was always something to steal his attention, particularly on a Thursday lunchtime . . .

In the heart of Soho, on Peter Street, is the Supreme store. Supreme is a fashion brand, founded in 1994 in New York city, that occupies the intersection between skateboard and hip-hop culture. Initially they built their brand specifically for skate kids, and this influenced everything from the layout of their first stores in New York to the type of clothing they designed. Their dominance in skate culture soon crossed over into hip-hop, and then, eventually, took hold in mainstream youth culture.

Supreme became and remains one of the most recognisable, and ripped-off, brands today. They found a core audience rooted in sub-culture, and amongst the coveted 'hypebeasts'. This audience is made up of the type of customers who emerge, whatever the weather, to buy their products and evangelise about them at length to anyone who might listen.

EXERCISE: What brands, in your opinion, are queue worthy and why?

....

....

....

....

....

....

....

....

....

....

As you set out to build a brand, have in mind who you want your core audience to be and make it your mission to understand exactly who they are, their attitudes, behaviours and needs.

You should understand your customers *intimately*. As over the top as that may sound, the brands that succeed are the ones that spend the time and do the work to figure out who their audience really are. This understanding means they can build a brand that makes things that their audience actually wants, communicate in a way their audience really understands, and respond to the changes in their audience's lives in a timely and effective manner.

CONNECT WITH YOUR COMMUNITY

Your core audience aren't just individuals. Think of them as a community of people that have an interest in your brand, share your values and believe in your purpose. In the age of the internet, having a core audience who behave like a community is a powerful asset.

This community will be the first in every queue, will shout the loudest for your brand on social media and will bring other people to your brand, without you asking them to.

Very few companies seem to understand the power of building a brand using the power of community, but those who do can grow very quickly. There have been some fantastic examples of brands who came out of nowhere and became huge, in part because of the power of the community they embraced.

NO SIGNAL – An online radio brand created during the Covid-19 lockdown of 2020, went from zero to 90k listeners, including musical trendsetters Burna Boy and Popcaan, in a matter of weeks. No Signal's success was due to its ability to connect with an engaged and passionate Black British Twitter community with its music gameshow format #NS10VS10.

RUN DEM CREW – A running brand founded by DJ, poet and writer Charlie Dark that has inspired thousands in London and around the globe, and grown rapidly as an internationally renowned brand. Run Dem Crew's success was powered by their ability to engage a local community of people brought together through their love of running.

We see time and time again that brands that listen, adapt and give back to their community tend to be the brands that gain the most passionate support from their community in return.

UNDERSTANDING YOUR AUDIENCE

Back in 2013, Damola left his first proper advertising agency job to join mobile fin-tech start-up, Osper, as the sixth member of their founding team. It was a chance to experience the world of start-ups at a time when London start-up culture was just about to blow up, but, more importantly, it was an opportunity to help build a banking brand with a genuine purpose.

Osper was built as a bank for young people, using technology to help them manage their money and give them financial freedom. Imagine Monzo, but for young people between eight and eighteen years old. What was special about Osper was that it had two audiences: young people who used the app and the card, and parents who used the app to put money on the card so that young people could spend money just as we adults do.

Thanks to this dual audience, it was important to build a brand that appealed to both parents and young people equally, but for different reasons. Catering to two audiences with different needs was no mean feat, so Osper had to really understand what these two audiences cared about, which was where Damola came in.

His job, as customer lead at this start-up, was to help the rest of the team understand more about their audiences as they built the brand.

Damola realised there were a range of things to focus on, from young people's relationship with money and their financial behaviour to how young people and parents used the app and card.

EXERCISE: What do you know about the audience you want to build your brand for?

....

....

....

....

....

....

....

....

....

Here are some methods you can use to understand your audience better:

I. SKETCH AN OUTLINE OF THEM

Your audience are complex people, so don't oversimplify them. There are four dimensions you can use to sketch a rough picture of who they are in your mind:

— **DEMOGRAPHIC INFORMATION (WHO THE AUDIENCE ARE)** – Information that relates to the characteristics of your audience, such as their age, gender, location, income etc

— **BEHAVIOURAL INFORMATION (HOW THE AUDIENCE BEHAVE)** – Information that relates to what people actually do, such as how often they use a product or service, what media they use and how they consume it

— **ATTITUDINAL INFORMATION (HOW THE AUDIENCE THINKS)** – Information that shows people's perception of your brand, product or service, such as customer satisfaction, product desirability etc

— **INTEREST-BASED INFORMATION (WHAT THEY CARE ABOUT)** – Information that tells you what your audience likes doing, such as sport, art, politics, all sorts

2. ADD SOME TEXTURE

Figuring out the demographic, behavioural, attitudinal and interest profile of an audience will heavily depend on your resources and the time you have available to you. Below are four of my favourite ways of colouring in between the lines and drawing a fuller picture of your audience.

DESK RESEARCH

You won't be the first person trying to understand the audience you want to learn more about. Here are some tools you can use to find insights about different audience groups.

— Think With Google: A resource that helps you understand shifts in consumer behaviours, needs and benefits.

— Reddit: An underrated resource if you want to find out what people are saying about a range of subjects in real time.

— Mintel: Reports from Mintel are fantastic, because they are both in-depth and broad, and they can give you a great top-line understanding of a subject area. The only downside is that they are pretty pricey.

- YouGov: Another hidden gem. YouGov conduct surveys of the UK population on a variety of different subjects. You can delve into their reports and find out what the public think about everything from fitness instructor Joe Wicks to how to stack your book shelf.

SOCIAL LISTENING

Social listening is basically observing the tweets, comments and other chat people have in public on social media platforms. The public conversations people have on social media platforms can give you a great insight into what people really think about a particular subject or brand. It's good because it's unprompted and can be an accurate representation of what people really think.

You can go on to Twitter or Reddit right now and search for a brand and see what people are saying about it.

SEE THE WORLD THROUGH YOUR AUDIENCE'S EYES

Desk research is fine, but nothing beats actually speaking to your audience. Get used to getting away from your desk to find out what they really think. If you can find people who are representative of your audience, take the time to speak with them; conduct one-to-one interviews or focus groups to probe and discuss the subject matter with them. This method often gives you the opportunity to ask questions that are specific to your brand, whilst also being able to ask general questions. The flexibility of this approach is where you really benefit.

Another method is spending time observing your audience in their day-to-day life. This is a really interesting way to get to the bottom of things, as it gives you the chance to see what's really going on without you prompting or interfering. As you observe, make notes about how they live and go about their day to day, and try to understand how your brand can solve problems they encounter or can add value to their life.

All of these methods should help you develop great insights about your audience that you can use to decide your brand's future strategy, development and communication.

3. DELVE DEEPER

Now you've got a better understanding of your audience at the general level, there may be more specific things you want to know. For those things, develop a hypothesis, i.e. a statement that expresses what you think is the case, then use the same research methods to prove or disprove it.

e.g. Hypothesis: If young people manage their money well between eight to eighteen years old, they are less likely to have financial problems between eighteen to thirty.

DEFINITION: WHAT IS AN INSIGHT?

Insight is thought that challenges what you thought you knew about a defined audience and gives you a deeper understanding of how that audience thinks and/or behaves. An insight can be developed from observation and data about human behaviour and attitudes.

AN EXAMPLE OF A BRAND-DEFINING INSIGHT

After an extensive study, the executives at Dove found that only 2 per cent of the women who participated considered themselves beautiful.

This insight inspired the award-winning Dove Beauty Sketches, a campaign that aimed to show women that they are more beautiful than they think they are.

Search YouTube: Dove Real Beauty Sketches

DECIDING WHAT AUDIENCE MAKES SENSE
FOR YOUR BRAND

As we established, you don't want your (core) audience to be *everyone* – you've got to make a choice. Thinking strategically about who to build your brand for is important. When thinking about who you're building for, go back to your brand 'why' – why you're creating/building this for them.

When we help people understand who their audience should be, we group them into four categories to try to determine which audience would be the most suitable for the brand to go after.

Is the audience:

— **LARGE AND OVERSERVED:** Lots of potential customers who are being targeted by other brands (e.g. people booking taxis via mobile apps)

— **LARGE AND UNDERSERVED:** Lots of potential customers who are not being targeted by other brands (e.g. people looking for meat alternatives)

— **SMALL AND UNDERSERVED:** Few potential customers who aren't being targeted by other brands (e.g. Nigerians looking for Nigerian restaurants in London)

- **SMALL AND OVERSERVED:** Few potential customers who are being targeted by other brands (e.g a small seaside town, with a fish and chip shop on every road)

EXERCISE: Who would you want your core audience and community to be?

....
....
....
....
....
....
....
....
....
....
....
....

TIP

Whichever audience you choose to build for, think about why your audience is the right one and if that audience is going to be sufficient to support the growth of your brand.

TAPPING INTO CULTURE

Culture is a term often used when brand marketers are trying to understand how to connect with a range of people. Let's define it for our purposes before we move on:

DEFINITION: CULTURE (NOUN) – 'The way of life, especially the general customs and beliefs, of a particular group of people at a particular time' -Cambridge Dictionary.

Brands have always looked to culture to find what's cool today or discover the next trend, because cultures are a hotbed of inspiration, ideas and creativity and have the power to propel brands from a niche to the mainstream.

However, tapping into 'culture' is not a guaranteed way of making your brand cool or compelling.

Culture is a way of life for people; it is sacred and should not be seen as a tool for a brand to exploit for financial gain. We all know the saying 'culture vultures' – an easy call out for brands that appropriate other people's cultures. As a brand, you should aspire to genuinely understanding a culture and its nuances. This level of understanding is what will make your brand relevant to your audience and inform how your brand behaves and communicates. Here are two different ways we've seen brands tap into culture and how.

YOU CAN REFLECT CULTURE:

By diving deep into a particular culture and learning about its nuances. Reflecting a particular culture in your brand can be subtle, or overt. When people see your brand, they should see what you are trying to mirror.

TESCO: FOOD LOVE STORIES CAMPAIGN – An advertising campaign all about making the food you love for the people that you love, and helping the British public discover new ingredients and recipes attached to real stories. This campaign reflected mainstream British food culture and depicted a cross-section of British society.

YOU CAN COMMENT ON CULTURE:

By having a clear point of view on a certain aspect of culture, or an issue that is important. Taking this approach opens your brand up to being defined by that position.

LED BY DONKEYS – A British campaign group that grew popular by commenting on British political culture and political issues. They connected with audiences because of their ability to comment on culture in a simple, uncomplicated and creative way.

FOUR PRINCIPLES TO REMEMBER ABOUT CULTURE

1. Spend time with the people that shape it – understand its nuances, especially if you're an outsider.

2. Give back in a meaningful way – don't just take, give back value and build a long-term and mutal relationship.

3. Be authentic and respectful in your portrayal – there's nothing worse than cultural stereotypes, be mindful you are not contributing to charactures and tropes.

---

4. Culture does not happen in a vacuum – you may be new to certain aspects of culture, but it existed before you came to it.

EXERCISE: Take a moment to reflect on what you have read and complete the table below. Use this as a summary of your brand story.

....

....

....

....

....

....

....

At (YOUR BRAND NAME) we believe (YOUR BRAND VALUES) and that is why we (YOUR PURPOSE).

We offer (YOUR PROPOSITION) for (YOUR AUDIENCE).

SHARING YOUR BRAND WITH THE WORLD

CHAPTER 7

GET THE EXPERIENCE RIGHT

Your brand is more than just a logo on a box, an advertisement to show your friends or the product you've been building. Your brand is an experience – made up of a number of 'touchpoints'.

TOUCHPOINTS: A touchpoint is a word that is used in marketing and design to describe a place where a customer can interact with your brand. That place can be physical or virtual, a person or an object.

Some of the most common touchpoints for a brand are:

— You and your team

— Your shop

— Your website

— Your social media presence

— Your advertising

— Your packaging

— Delivery of your product or service

Every interaction a customer has with any of your brand's touchpoints will influence their perception of it. Any Apple user only needs to think back to when they opened the box containing their first iPhone to see how Apple were capable of influencing brand perception from the unboxing experience alone. In the book of his life by Walter Issacson, former Chief Design Officer of Apple Sir Jony Ive said:

> 'Steve and I spend a lot of time on the packaging. I love the process of unpacking something. You design a ritual of unpacking to make the product feel special. Packaging can be theatre, it can create a story.'

Steve Jobs and Jony Ive understood that each interaction mattered and designed the hell out of every single opportunity. The result is an experience people admire almost as much as the technology itself.

Similarly, a great customer experience from the get-go wasn't a 'nice to have' when Damola helped launch Osper – it was a 'must have'. Osper wanted trust and satisfaction to start building from the very first moment a customer came into contact with the brand. Starter packs came with a welcome note signed personally by each of the founding members, and on occasion Damola would even hand-deliver the starter packs in the early days. Not only did this delight young customers, but it also helped Osper build a unique relationship with them.

The great thing is, if you know what your brand's touchpoints are and understand the types of interactions a consumer will have, you can design an experience that leaves customers satisfied. On the flip side, if you don't know what your brand's touchpoints are or don't understand how people interact with them, you have no control over the consumer experience and will soon start receiving tweets from disgruntled customers.

Now, we aren't suggesting you create an Apple-type customer experience at every touchpoint or start hand-delivering your product, but what we are suggesting is you take the time to map out the consumer experience and think about how to optimise it.

EXERCISE:

1. Imagine a person came across your brand for the first time through an advertisement on Instagram and decided to purchase a product.

Describe every interaction they would have with your brand, from finding out about your brand to receiving the product. List your touch points in order of the journey the consumer would take.

....

....

2. How would they describe their experience at each touchpoint?

....

....

3. What could you do to improve that experience?

....

....

DON'T LET THEM FORGET YOU

Remember when we were talking about making people give a shit and care about your brand? Another part of this is ensuring that your brand sticks in people's memories, whenever they experience it. Bear in mind people's natural forgetfulness. Our careers in agencies have taught us that nothing we do is useful if people don't remember it.

Here are a few ways to make sure your brand is easy to remember, when you finally decide to tell the world who you are.

Take a moment to think about a brand you remember from your youth. What did your memory churn out? You probably don't remember all the details, but you might remember some very specific things – the slogan, a logo, a catchy jingle. Damola's, for instance, brought back Tango – 'You know when you've been Tango'd' – and Weetabix – 'Have you had your Weetabix?'

It's no accident that there are things you remember about certain brands. We've both been a part of advertising meeting rooms crammed full of people thinking: 'What cues can we design that will help audiences remember the brand for years and years to come?'

These 'cues' are called distinctive brand assets, and brands design them to be noticed, to be remembered and to make them stand apart from other brands. You may not know it, but you're surrounded by them. You're probably wearing one on a T-shirt now.

For example, which brand comes to mind when you see these images and words?

Three stripes.
Every Little Helps.
Vorsprung durch Technik.
Just Do It.

There are a range of brand elements that can be a distinctive brand asset, such as: colours, slogans, music, sounds, jingles, style of advertising, logo or symbols, characters, celebrities or pack shapes.

EXERCISE: Look at the brand elements above and make a list of what you have so far, keeping in mind you don't need to have them all. Consider which of these will be your distinctive assets, and decide where you are going to use them across your communications and channels.

For any of these elements to be considered a distinctive asset, it has to 'evoke the brand' in the mind of the consumer. Basically, a consumer should be able to see the asset and instinctively associate it with your brand.

A distinctive asset needs to be well-known, which means you will need to commit to using it consistently in and on all your communications and channels. This, in turn, takes time, so make sure you're not chopping and changing these assets frequently.

MAKE YOUR BRAND EXPERIENCE CONSISTENT

On the occasions a brand bolts out the gates gracefully, the thing that impresses us most is how considered and consistent its brand identity is. Brand identity is what the brand looks and feels like to the outside world. Your brand identity consists of a number of elements:

— Brand name

— Logo

— Key colours/colour palette

— Fonts and typography

— Photographic style

It's your identity that will tie your touchpoints to your brand. Designing a brand identity is not as simple as getting a designer to create a logo. A considered, consistent and coherent brand identity needs to reflect what the brand is about, its values and positioning. For example, if you've agreed that your brand is a premium brand, your brand identity shouldn't be plastered with Comic Sans.

These are the tell-tale signs of a great brand identity:

— It's distinctive: the identity feels like it belongs to that brand and that brand alone. Regardless of what you may think of Virgil Abloh's Off-White brand, when you see those block capitals emblazoned on a trainer or on Drake's plane, you know it's a Virgil situation.

— It's flexible: the identity can work across any touchpoint – big or small, on or offline. Take a brand like Spotify, for example, whose footprint is predominantly online, but which has a brand identity that worked equally well in its recent highly visible end-of-year outdoor advertising campaign.

— It's consistent: the identity is used across all touchpoints in the same way. Wherever you see the Nike Swoosh logo, the Swoosh is the Swoosh – it's not inverted, it's not messed with. Inconsistency creates confusion, and confusion does not create success.

There are some easy steps you can take to make sure your identity hits all of these points:

— Do an audit of other brands in your category or market to make sure your brand looks distinctive and not like a copycat. List all the other brands in the same category as yours. Take screenshots of their brand assets, such as the logo and front page of the website, and place them next to each other to see where the similarities and differences are.

— Stress-test the design elements on various assets, such as an Instagram post, a poster, or website banner, to see how flexible your brand identity is and where it is unusable.

— Create rules and guidelines for how elements can and cannot be used, so anyone working on your brand will be able to keep the identity consistent.

CHAPTER 8

GET YOUR COMMUNICATIONS RIGHT

The foundation of your brand is its purpose, vision, proposition and values. Without these, your brand is likely to change direction every time the wind blows. Your foundation is irrelevant if you can't channel it into effective communication, telling the world what your brand is all about. What you say and how you say it has the power to give your brand power in people's minds. If done well, it can make a great first and lasting impression. For some, this will be the fun bit. The bit where you get to bring the brand to life. However, always make sure that what you communicate refers back to your foundations and stays true to them.

WHY AND WHAT SHOULD YOU COMMUNICATE

Why should your brand communicate? If you haven't thought about this question, now is the time. There are many good answers to this question, but two stand out to us.

— **TO CREATE DEMAND FOR YOUR BRAND LONG-TERM** – This means getting people to actually want the product or service the brand offers.

— **TO CONVERT THE DEMAND YOU'VE CREATED** – This means getting people to actually buy the product or service your brand offers.

Without these two dynamics, your brand cannot be successful. We'll break down some advice on how to create and convert demand, but first have a go at this exercise.

EXERCISE: Imagine you are a record label brand, with one artist on the roster that no one has heard of.

1. How would you use communications to create demand for this artist?

....

....

2. What would be your main message and what communications channels would you use?

....

....

3. How would you use communications to get people to buy that artist's first single?

....

....

....

That exercise should have been pretty fun to complete, but should also demonstrate that this isn't rocket science, and there are many things you will already know about how to use communications to create and convert demand.

PRINCIPLES FOR COMMUNICATION THAT CREATES DEMAND

PRINCIPLE 1: HAVE AN INTERESTING POINT OF VIEW

The number one rule for communicating with your audience is, 'Don't be boring.' Your brand is in a battle for a consumer's attention, fighting it out with brands that have more money and experience than you. If you're stepping into the battle with limited resources and experience, you need to rely on different weapons to win. You may have a smaller budget and less experience, but we are sure you can be more interesting.

So if you want to win attention and create demand for your brand, have something interesting to say to your audience. Something that takes your 'proposition' from a one-dimensional message describing what you do, to an 'idea' that fully conveys what your brand is about. Making a leap from the proposition to an idea isn't simple, it requires a tablespoon full of insight about your audience, and a whole heap of creative thinking.

Brands you'll recognise have made that leap and have created memorable ideas through trade mark slogans that convey what that brand is all about. For example:

SNICKERS – YOU'RE NOT YOU WHEN YOU'RE HUNGRY®

SKITTLES – TASTE THE RAINBOW®

WEETABIX – HAVE YOU HAD YOUR WEETABIX?®

If you have an interesting idea that encapsulates what your brand is about, how you communicate it can take many different forms. It can be a tweet, a roadside poster, or a sixty-second television advert. Whatever form they take, the best brand ideas are capable of stirring up the strongest of emotions within people, emotions that linger in the form of memories in the corner of people's minds. What's more impressive is that every now and again, the brain will pull that memory from its dusty corners and place the idea of that brand smack bang in the centre of its attention. If that happens to your brand, trust us, you've won the battle.

Big enduring brand ideas like 'Taste the rainbow' and 'You're not you when you're hungry' are few and far between these days, so don't worry if you can't create something similar. You don't necessarily need one for demand-creating communications, but you still need to be interesting. Imagine your brand was a person walking into a party of strangers; what would your brand say to this group of people, that will make them ask, 'Who's your mate? You better invite them to the next party!'

— Have an interesting point of view on what your brand does and offers to people.

— Express that point of view as creatively as possible.

PRINCIPLE 2: REACH AS MANY PEOPLE AS POSSIBLE

Creating demand is as much about how many people you can communicate with as it is about what you communicate. When you are trying to create demand, think about how you can get your communication in front of as many people as possible with the budget you have.

This may mean starting in digital and investing a small budget on buying advertisements on social media to begin with.

The result you want is to have as many people as possible being aware of and interested in your brand

and what it offers, and feeling connected to what you do, and why you do it.

PRINCIPLE 3: USE EMOTION

It has been proven by numerous marketing experts that communications that use emotion are more effective in the long term than rational communications. Injecting emotion into your communications creates lasting memories in people's minds, that influence their purchasing decisions in the future. Emotion is not one dimensional, there are many different 'emotions' that you can employ such as humour, sadness or excitement. Choose the one that is appropriate for your brand and what you're trying to communicate. The alternative is communications that are straight and very rational but forgettable and therefore not as effective.

PRINCIPLES FOR COMMUNICATIONS THAT CONVERT DEMAND

PRINCIPLE I: TELL PEOPLE WHAT THEY ARE GOING TO GET

If you've created some awareness and interest in your brand, the only way you are going to convince people to part with their money for your product or services is by targeting them with a message that lets them know how your brand is going to benefit them. You can do this with messages that balance your brand's functional and emotional benefits.

1. **FUNCTIONAL BENEFIT** – What feature or attributes does your brand offer to a consumer?

   — E.g. Brand X

     — Saves you money

     — Keeps you connected

     — Helps you stay healthy

     — Simplifies your life

2. **EMOTIONAL BENEFIT** – What emotional pay-off or reward can a consumer expect from your brand?

   — E.g. Brand X

     — Makes you feel optimistic about the future

     — Makes you feel loved

     — Makes you feel in control of your life

     — Makes you feel like you stand out in the crowd

EXERCISE:

1. What are the benefits of your brand's product or service?

Functional benefit:

....

Emotional benefit:

....

2. How would you turn this into a Tweet convincing someone to buy your product or service?

Tweet:

....

PRINCIPLE 2: TARGET THE MESSAGE AT THE RIGHT PEOPLE

You've created demand by getting your brand in front of as many people as possible. To convert that demand, your brand should focus on speaking to people who are already aware and interested, and are in the frame of mind to consider your brand and buy your product or service.

At this stage it's best to use media channels where you can speak to people as personally as possible, such as email and targeted social media advertisements. The assets you create for these channels should be as relevant to the consumer as you can make them, with the resources and information you have.

Damola's favourite example of targeted communications that encouraged him to consider and buy comes from Danish headphone brand AIAIAI. After watching a YouTube video from music channel COLORS Berlin, Damola decided to search what headphones the artists in the video were wearing. They happened to be these modular headphones made by AIAIAI.

That search was all it took for AIAIAI to know that Damola was aware and might be interested in their brand and product. A day later, he received a targeted Instagram ad just before Black Friday, advertising their headphones, which also featured one of his favourite DJs, Benji B.

Even though he's spent years working in advertising, Damola is always amazed when brands are able to communicate with him so seamlessly. Within a matter of three days, he'd gone from not knowing about these headphones to buying a pair in a Black Friday deal, all because they were able to create demand for their brand and product and convert that demand, using communications.

WHERE SHOULD YOU COMMUNICATE?

Some of the best channels on which to build your brand are still TV, billboards or print media, but, as you're starting out, it's unlikely that you will be able to afford these.

Thanks to the internet, there are more and more places to reach people on a smaller budget. However, because of this, you need to take a long, hard think about where you need to be in order to create and convert demand without breaking the bank.

DON'T BE EVERYWHERE AT ONCE

When it comes to digital, you don't need to be everywhere at once: prioritise the channels you use based on the behaviour of your audience now and how you think they will behave in the future.

— Go where the majority of your audience is and where it's active.

— Keep an eye on channels where a minority of your audience is but where they are also active.

— Ignore channels where there are small numbers of your audience and low activity.

GO WHERE YOUR AUDIENCE ARE

To figure out where your audience is and how active it is online, there is a fantastic tool called Global Web Index.

Global Web Index can tell you a lot of things about your audience, but it's particularly good at telling you which digital platforms people are using, how often they use them and what they use them for in general.

GIVE EACH CHANNEL A SPECIFIC ROLE

Think about the way you use digital and social media channels. We're sure the photos you post on Instagram are different to the photos you use for LinkedIn. If you use your personal channels differently, you should definitely use your brand channels differently. When defining what the role for each channel is, think about how people behave on those channels and how your behaviour as a brand can play into that.

EXERCISE:

What channels are you planning to use to reach your audience?

....

....

What are you going to use each channel for?

....

....

WHEN SHOULD YOU COMMUNICATE?

As important as it is for your brand to communicate, it still stands true that, if you have nothing good to say, say nothing at all. If your brand is just starting out, then hang on to that advice, because in this case talk isn't cheap. In fact, it can cost a fair amount to communicate with your audience, so when you do, make sure you have a real reason to.

As a general principle, when you do communicate, you will need to invest in media to make sure it reaches people. The amount you spend can vary; you can get started with as little as a few hundred pounds in digital. Work within the budget you have. Long gone are the days where you could post something on Twitter or Facebook and expect lots of people to see it, unless you've spent some money on boosting its reach.

We remember the days before social media, when there wasn't a constant stream of information from everyone and their mum. It will be tempting to communicate whenever you have an urge to say something to your audience but do your best to resist that urge. The next time your instinct tells you to post something on behalf of your brand, put your phone down and pick up a pen and paper, go analogue and map out the year. Plot all the moments in the year, month or even week ahead of when you plan to communicate with your audience, and why those moments matter for your brand. You can do this on a regularly timed basis. It will give structure to your brand's communications and give you peace of mind.

TIP

Before you crack on with any comms, we think it's useful to go through a short checklist that will help focus your attention and clarify why you're communicating, who you're communicating with, what the focus of your communications will be, what channels you're using and when you are planning to communicate.

— *Do you want to create or convert demand?*

— *Will creating and converting demand grow the market or grow your share of the market?*

— *Are you telling people about your brand or your product?*

— *Who are you trying to reach: current or new customers?*

— *What channels will you be using to reach them?*

— *When are you planning to communicate and what difference might this make?*

CHAPTER 9

GETTING IT RIGHT IN DIGITAL

Now more than ever, digital is the place where you'll start your brand's journey. It's accessible for the masses and low cost or even free – a place where you can test the waters and build a following organically.

But it's worth remembering that people's attention spans are shorter than ever before, with streams of content at the tips of our fingers: feeds, carousels, Netflix, tweets, TikToks – we could keep going for pages on end. In short, the likelihood of people remembering your brand amongst an endless and constant stream of content is low.

Niran has spent the last five years helping brands build creative campaigns and optimise their already existing campaigns on Facebook and Instagram. With that in mind, the next couple of sections provide his creative considerations and tips for launching your brand's presence online.

BRILLIANT BASICS

Your website and social media accounts are most likely the first places your consumer will encounter your brand. You've already probably produced a look and feel for your brand and product, and it's crucial you translate this across to your online presence as well. Some simple but important tips include:

- **CONSISTENCY IS KEY:** Find a name that can be the same across both your website and social media accounts.

- **GET YOUR WEBSITE SET UP:** Everyone will always go and search your brand on Google and the website is nearly always guaranteed to be the first point of contact from there. It's the shopfront that they see before taking a closer look inside so it's important to be able to convey the message of your brand in a clear and appealing way.

- **JOIN THE COMMUNITY:** Find out where your consumer is spending the most time online. Meet them where they are, building relevant content and engaging within the community. You have to actively engage in conversations, and not just be a one-way participant.

- **UNDERSTAND THE FORMAT:** Whether it is for a feed, stories or anything else – understand the user behaviour for that format and build creative content with that in mind.

USING INSTAGRAM EFFECTIVELY

When Niran first started at IG, they were just launching all their business tools, and brands were still in the early stages of figuring out how to use the platform to connect with their consumers. Many weren't sure what to do and everyone wanted to find the trick for overnight growth.

Let's be real – there is no secret recipe to Instagram success, but here are a few creative considerations and tips, especially when it comes to advertising:

— **DON'T BE AFRAID TO BRING YOUR BRAND TO THE FRONT:** People scroll or swipe past after a few short seconds, so it's crucial to have branding up front so people immediately know what they're looking at.

— **MAKE IT SNAPPY:** Land the message in the first few seconds. If your content is long, think about how you're going to grab people's attention to keep them watching. Think text overlays, branding up front or even re-editing the whole clip to bring the end to the beginning.

— **SHOW OFF YOUR PRODUCT:** Your product is your key message – don't shy away from posting a simple image of it. You don't always need a beautifully shot cinematic sequence about your brand. If the product is 'dope', get that in front of your consumers' eyes.

— **USE METRICS AND INSIGHTS:** You get real-time insights on every piece of content that you put out on your brand's profile, meaning it's easy to track what is and isn't working. See what engages best with your audience and keep tweaking as you create more content.

EXERCISE: Imagine your social channel is a person and ask yourself:

What type of person are they?

....

What do they stand for?

....

What are they into?

....

This will help develop a content theme and pillars for your brand, especially if you're struggling with what content to share on your brand channels.

MORE MOBILE-FIRST CRAFT

As a small business owner, we understand your time is already spread thin. You're generally either building the business or product, dealing with finances, confronting the legal side and so on. Which all goes to say that building bespoke creative content for each social media channel often isn't the best use of your time. Instead, there are several mobile apps out there that help speed things up, with templates to optimise efficiently across multiple platforms. Here's a few, to save you time:

— **OVER** – Use templates, tools and effects to make your brand and personal projects stand out.

— **MOJO** – Video templates with kinetic typography and motion graphics. Instantly makes your creative content look more slick and professional.

— **VSCO** – Niran's go-to app for photo-editing on the fly. Lots of film-style filters that can enhance your photos.

— **UNFOLD** – Lots of creative stories templates.

TIP

As Damola mentions earlier on, getting your brand experience consistent is key, so you'll hopefully already have a typeface that you use for your brand. You can airdrop fonts from your Mac to your phone so that you can access them within the apps mentioned above for asset creation.

REFLECTING ON THE JOURNEY

CHAPTER 10

EMBRACE FEEDBACK AND FAILURE

If you're in the process of creating a brand, you already know that not everything will always go as you'd hoped. Failure is probably one of the hardest things you're going to have to face. But that shouldn't put you off.

The reality is that 20 per cent of small businesses shut their doors permanently within the first twelve months. However, what you should take from this statement is that the majority of new brands survive and go on to be successful, even if they encounter difficulties. Yes, the path to success will be bumpy, but you'll be able to ride out most of those bumps.

FEEDBACK IS YOUR FRIEND

Damola clearly remembers the dread he'd feel before asking his boss to review his creative briefs. He'd be terrified that his boss would rip them apart and he'd have to start again. Eventually, though, Damola realised the anticipation of his boss's feedback made him consider all the angles, making his work as bulletproof as possible, and also that the actual feedback usually made his work better. The same was true when sharing business ideas with people.

That feeling of dread never quite goes away and feedback always feels personal, especially if you've invested time and effort in something. But we'd rather have that feeling than create an idea that flops because we didn't bother to ask for someone else's opinion.

In our experience, the path to success is much easier if you seek and embrace feedback along the way. Sometimes feedback can feel painful, but, trust us, it's a gift, no matter how harsh it may feel at the time. So actively seek it out.

The best time to ask for feedback is when you can still do something with the opinions you receive. We'd advise you to get feedback while you're still crafting your brand and its story, designing your experience and developing your communications.

Be methodical about your approach to feedback

1. **DECIDE WHAT YOU WANT TO LEARN FROM THE FEEDBACK**
   - e.g. I want to understand which proposition is more attractive for my audience.

2. **CREATE DIFFERENT SCENARIOS TO TEST WITH PEOPLE**
   - e.g. Proposition 1: a phone for people who have no time for technology *vs* Proposition 2: a phone without the distractions.

3. **SELECT THE RIGHT AUDIENCE TO GET FEEDBACK FROM**

— e.g. I want to get feedback from a cross-section of my target audience and my personal board of directors.

4. **DECIDE ON WHAT YOU WANT TO DO WITH THE FEEDBACK BEFORE YOU RECEIVE IT**

— e.g. I will use the feedback to choose the proposition that I will build my brand around.

You will hear a lot of different things from different people. Ultimately, it's up to you to decide what you use and what you discard.

FEEDBACK FROM CUSTOMERS

If you're really comfortable with feedback and with embracing potential failure, get your brand into people's hands as soon as you can. You can do that by forming a 'founding customer group' – a small group of people who fit your audience profile and are prospective future customers. This group should be small but representative of your audience. Put your brand's product and service directly in their hands first. Get them to use it. It's important that your brand doesn't exist in a bubble for two reasons:

1. You can get honest feedback from a range of people before releasing it to a wider audience. This means you can fix any problems you may have discovered, or optimise the experience for future customers.

2. If the brand's product or service meets and exceeds people's expectations, people are likely to start talking about it and building buzz and interest before you've made it widely available. This word of mouth helps to create demand for your brand, at very low cost.

PIVOTING YOUR PLAN

Failure is rarely a single, unexpected event in the life of a brand. More likely, it'll be a series of missteps that cause you to fail. The good news is that this means that you are likely to have a number of moments where you can intervene and course-correct before getting to that point.

If you are encountering problems or consistently missing your objectives, the first thing you have to do is dig into the available data to find out why. This could be operational or financial data, or insights you gather from speaking to consumers. Somewhere in the weeds will be the information you need to figure out why the brand is struggling.

Here are some questions you should be asking yourself:

— Are you meeting your strategic goals and objectives? If not, why?

— If your brand continues to miss its targets, how long can it survive?

— Are you meeting your audience's needs? If not, why?

— What does your audience want that you aren't currently providing?

These are difficult questions to ask and you may not like the answers, but if you aren't hitting your goals or meeting your audience's needs, you need to understand why. In most instances, these things are connected, and if you cannot resolve one or the other, it's likely that your brand won't survive very long, and you'll need to think about how you pivot or wrap up your brand.

Even the most famous brands in the world experienced difficulties on their journey, but they pivoted and bounced back stronger:

— Before Twitter was a news juggernaut, it was a podcasting service called Odeo.

— Before YouTube was synonymous with video, it was a video-based online dating service.

— Before Instagram was the online home for photos, it was a location-based app called Burbn.

If you are seeing less than positive signals, don't immediately lose hope. This may just be the sign that a different path awaits your brand.

CHECK YOURSELF BEFORE YOU WRECK YOURSELF

To intercept potential fails, you need to be on top of your KPIs (key performance indicators) and objectives. It's important you measure your performance at regular intervals (and not just at the end of the year), because you don't want to risk it being too late to save a deteriorating situation or make the most of a great opportunity. As a general rule, the more often you measure your performance, the more opportunities you have to optimise your activity and turn a loss into a win.

A starting point is to set up a system that measures and reports on two levels:

STRATEGIC REPORTING

These reports measure the overall health of your business and should measure how you are performing against your goals and objectives. Review this at least once a month.

OPERATIONAL REPORTING

These reports measure the day-to-day activity of the business and should measure how certain operations and functions (such as finance, production or sales) are performing. Review these at least once a month, if not once a fortnight.

ACKNOWLEDGING A LOSS WITH PRIDE

As a culture, we are terrified of failure, desperately ducking and diving to avoid it at every turn. Don't get us wrong: trying to avoid a loss is not a bad thing – I can't imagine anyone setting off with failure as their ultimate objective. But constantly swerving just to save face can be counterproductive.

Loss-aversion is a mentality that can negatively affect decision-making and put you in a position where you continuously do things to avoid losing, rather doing everything you can to win. There is a difference. When advising those who are unsure of starting a brand because of the fear of failure, we ask them four questions:

- Are you scared because you're afraid of what others will think if you fail?
  - If the answer to this question is yes, imagine how you would feel if someone else develops this idea instead of you.

- Are you scared because no one has done it before?
  - If the answer to this question is yes, imagine the upside if you are the first to crack it.

- Are you scared because other people have done it before, and you don't think you can do it better?
  - If the answer to the question is yes, consider how multiple chicken shops, selling exactly the same thing, on the same street, manage. If they can do it, you can too.

- Are you scared because you may fail?
  - If the answer to the question is yes, imagine what you can learn in the process.

MANAGING RISK

When building a brand, there will be decisions you take that yield great returns but have high risk. In other words, they can only be taken if you are comfortable with acknowledging a loss as well as celebrating a potential win.

There's a lot that can be learned from failure. Rather than asking, 'Why did this fail?', ask yourself, 'What can I learn from what happened?' Take a moment to get to grips with the lessons from your losses.

— What are the losses you've experienced?

— What did you learn from the losses?

— What would you do differently in a similar situation next time?

CHAPTER II

Happiness over Hustle

WORK-LIFE BALANCE

Niran's views on work-life balance were heavily impacted by the book *The Purpose Driven Life*, by Rick Warren, which he read in his early twenties. There's a line in it about time that he still thinks about even now: 'Time is your most precious gift because you only have a set amount of it. Time is the greatest gift that you can give anyone.' When you're young, it's easy to take time for granted, but when you're starting a brand or career, time becomes your most precious commodity. Most people spend at least forty hours a week working, and probably more if they're setting up their own thing on the side.

We're living in the era of 'hustle porn', or the fetishisation of extremely long work hours. In other words, the idea that working longer hours equals success. It's a common term used across social media, usually accompanied by quotes to inspire you to 'grind' and 'hustle hard' for your dreams. Work ethic is certainly essential for success, but working yourself too hard is damaging to your health and wellbeing. And, get this, it doesn't actually lead to increased productivity.

DEFINE SUCCESS FOR YOURSELF

Following your passion and striving to make your brand or career successful doesn't mean giving up everything else in your life. That will only lead to burnout and stop you being able to perform at your best. Define what success means to you from the outset so you don't lose yourself in the hustle and do a disservice to your brand and business. For example, success for Niran is now defined by being able to do his job to the best of his ability as well as being a great father and husband at home.

MAKE TIME FOR THE THINGS THAT ENERGISE YOU

In the days before marriage and fatherhood, it was always outside Niran's nine-to-five that he made time for Yin&Yang, meaning he would run home and get into side-hustle zone. It wouldn't have been a success if it hadn't focused on things that energised him and his co-founder, such as being able to explore new music, restaurants, launches and so on. Immersing himself in these worlds gave him the energy he needed to keep putting the work in.

Nowadays, Niran's energy comes from his family. After his daughter was born, his priorities naturally shifted. He does what he can to provide for her financially through work, but he also wants to get his ass back home to be a present father. That's what keeps him grounded and that balance is what defines success for him.

TYPES OF ACTIVITIES AND PLACES THAT MIGHT ENERGISE YOU

— Making time for friends and family

— Meditation

— Sleep

— Sport and fitness

— Arts and craft, simply creating for your own self-expression and not for business reasons

---

LOOKING AFTER YOURSELF

Everyone has their own way of energising themselves. It could be yoga, meditation, a HIIT class or even a long morning walk or a coffee ritual. Niran rediscovered his a few years back when his wife was pregnant and he made it his goal to get back into shape before he became a dad. Now, almost two years on, a morning workout is still a key part of his work day, and he can't start without it. It's his 'me time', an opportunity to clear his head and release a few endorphins in the process.

TIP:

— *Keep it at the same hour every day, i.e. don't let yourself start/finish without it. For Niran, that means waking up at 5 a.m. for his early commute followed by a workout.*

— *Turn it into a habit over time.*

— *Switch it up if it becomes monotonous.*

ENJOY THE FRUITS OF YOUR LABOUR

No high-demand job or business venture is worth more than your health, even when you're passionate about what you do. While working hard to 'make it' or get that next promotion, it's important to take breaks, reassess your priorities and enjoy the fruits of your labour. Why work so hard if you can't enjoy what you've earned? Don't forget to treat yourself – whatever that means to you. It could be a holiday, a dinner with loved ones, or simply a new video game to escape into.

SHARING IS CARING

Building a brand may feel like a lonely pursuit and you have probably carried plenty more on your own shoulders than you knew you could. But don't do this alone. In his final year of university, Damola ran in the annual student elections for a chance to be one of the six people leading the student body that year. The process required building a personal brand that people could trust and believe in, getting people to care about an election and getting people to vote. He had to apply many of the principles you've read about in this book, whilst attempting to win the vote. Campaigning was relentless but was made infinitely better because of the friends that rallied around to share the load, get out the vote and offer support as energy waned. The support they were able to give in the tough times not only helped take him across the line to victory but helped him throughout his year as a sabbatical officer.

During your own experience don't forget the people around you. They are not only invested in the success of your brand but they are invested in your happiness too. Don't hesitate to reach out and share your concerns, your needs and thoughts as you embark on this journey.

CHAPTER 12

PaY
iT
FORWaRD

PRACTICAL WAYS TO PAY IT FORWARD

'WHEN YOU LEARN, YOU TEACH. WHEN YOU GET, YOU GIVE.'

The aphorism above is one of the very first things that Niran noted down after watching Maya Angelou's episode of Oprah's *Masterclass* series, and it's been a staple of his iCloud notes since 2009. 'Paying it forward' means repaying someone's kindness with good deeds aimed at someone else. He's felt the effect of others paying it forward throughout his career. For example, when he first started out with Yin&Yang at university, so many people made time for him, sharing words of wisdom, insight and even letting him interview them for his dissertation. It felt only right for him to do the same for the next generation, especially for those from under-represented backgrounds. Remember that breaking the glass ceiling gives you an opportunity to take others with you.

We've all sat in conferences and listened to talks on diversity and inclusion and wondered how we can make a difference. Here are some ways to make a real impact:

- **MENTORSHIP** – Even if you're just starting out, you've already got experience you can pass to someone younger. If you're struggling to find a way to get started, there are plenty of organisations and universities that have alumni mentorship programmes. One organisation in London is the Creative Mentor Network, which assigns mentors from the creative industries to young people from lower socio-economic backgrounds not fully represented in the industry. Niran was a trustee on the board of CMN for two years to help them with their mission to broaden access and opportunities for a more diverse talent base in the UK creative industry.

- **RECRUITMENT** – Recruiting for roles within your team or organisation is a great way to invest in someone and give back.

- **INTERNSHIPS** – The internship that Niran did at WeAreSocial completely changed his career path and outlook on the industry. It's worthwhile checking to see if your employer has an internship scheme in place and if there are people within your network you can put forward for it. Interns are more than just the coffee errand boy/girl, and it's an opportunity for them to gain invaluable experience.

— **REFERRALS** – While internships are often the best route to bring younger, inexperienced people in, referrals are the next level up. Most large companies have referral programmes. Don't forget that referrals are a big ask, as it puts the referee's reputation on the line. We personally only refer people who we trust and who we've worked with already in some capacity.

— **SHARING KNOWLEDGE** – There are countless ways to share knowledge and pass on insights from your journey: hosting live events, going on a podcast, or simply talking to someone over a coffee. Don't be afraid to put yourself out there in order to connect and build community. Two years back, Niran spoke at a conference targeted at young people looking to get into the creative industry. After the event, a young guy came up to him to say that he quit his business degree, had spent a month attending similar events, and Niran was the first person he'd seen on a stage who looked like him. And all that took on Niran's part was an hour out of his week.

— **SOCIAL IMPACT** – Last but by no means least, brands today are expected to give back to their communities. Many consumers believe a lot of brands' social awareness campaigns are mere lip service, meaning that, more than ever, people want follow-through when it comes to a brand's actions. A great example of a brand that does this is the shoe brand TOMS. They've donated over 60 million pairs of shoes to children in need around the world, and they've helped the visually impaired by providing prescription glasses, medical treatments and more. Not every brand needs to think global, however, so ask yourself: what can you give back to your local community through your brand?

THROWING DOWN THE LADDER

If you're someone further down the road of setting up your own brand, there is no doubt you understand the long-term potential in taking the path less trodden, and will have learned more than your fair share of lessons. These teachings are not only valuable for you and your brand's growth – they are also invaluable to people like an eighteen-year-old Niran or Damola, interested in building their first brand.

So see this as an opportunity to throw down the ladder. Help others navigate the system, with the knowledge and experience you have acquired. You may think you don't have the time or energy, but there are two very good reasons why you should seriously consider it:

— **YOU'LL LEARN NEW LESSONS:** As you help people on the way up, they will show you things that might make you feel old but are incredibly beneficial, such as a new app you've never heard of but which is popular with your target audience, or a new way of working that could make your life easier.

— **A DIFFERENT WAY TO SOLVE PROBLEMS:** Speaking to someone at a different point in their trajectory, with different experiences, will offer you a different perspective on the same problem.

Whenever we've mentored someone, the experience has always been a two-way street: yes, you give a lot, but you get back much more.

CONCLUSION

When we both started out in this industry, we never thought all our experiences would lead to a book. We went from colleagues to co-authors just like that. We hope the lessons we've learnt over the years have broadened your personal knowledge on building your own brand and helped you get started. Here are a few closing thoughts about everything that we've learnt during the process of writing this book, which you can apply to what you're going to create.

TALK IS CHEAP, YOU ACTUALLY HAVE TO DO – We wanted this book to be practical, not another title full of inspiration with no space for application. The best way to learn is by doing. Getting your brand out there is the first step – you don't need anyone's permission; you'll learn by starting today.

PUT PEOPLE FIRST – We've been lucky enough to be friends for years, and also work and build with some incredible people along the way. We cannot underplay the role good people will play in the success of what you do. At every opportunity put people at the centre. The journey is as much about them as it is you.

BE BRAVE – No one said this was easy, but it is brave. Starting a brand – especially now – is an incredibly brave thing to do but that shouldn't stop once it's launched. You'll need bravery every step of the way – when you're faced with easy options, and difficult ones too.

POTENTIAL IS POWERFUL – There are people creating brands from their bedrooms that reverberate around the world in weeks. Anything is possible with graft, understanding and some humility too. What you're creating has the potential to be just as impactful and incredible.

Good luck!

appendix

p. 7 DJ Khaled, Drake, Lil Wayne, Rick Ross, 'No New Friends' (Republic Music, We The Best Music, Young Money, Cash Money Records, 2013)

p. 28 Gladwell, Malcolm, *Outliers: The Story of Success* (Penguin, 2009)

p. 30 Dweck, Carol S, *Mindset: Changing The Way You Think to Fulfil Your Potential* (Ballantine Books, 2007)

p. 45 In the UK, NIKE and the Nike Swoosh logo together and separately, and JUST DO IT are trade marks of Nike Innovate C.V.

TESLA is a registered trade mark of Tesla. Inc.

INNOCENT is a registered trade mark of Fresh Trading Limited.

FENTY BEAUTY is a registered trade mark of Roraj Trade LLC.

p. 49 In the UK, MCDONALD'S is a registered trade mark of McDonald's International Property Company, Ltd.

p. 52 UBER is a registered trade mark of Uber Technologies, Inc.

SOUNDCLOUD is a registered trade mark of SoundCloud Ltd.

PATCH is a registered trade mark of Patch Gardens Limited.

p. 87 Isaacson, Walter, *Steve Jobs* (Simon & Schuster, September 2015)

p. 90 In the UK, TANGO and YOU KNOW WHEN YOU'VE BEEN TANGO'D are trade marks of Britvic Brands LLP.

WEETABIX and HAVE YOU HAD YOUR WEETABIX? are registered trade marks of Weetabix Limited.

p. 99 YOU'RE NOT YOU WHEN YOU'RE HUNGRY is a registered EU trade mark of WM. Wrigley JR. Company

TASTE THE RAINBOW is a registered EU trade mark of WM. Wrigley JR. Company

WEETABIX and HAVE YOU HAD YOUR WEETABIX? are registered trade marks of Weetabix Limited.

p. 130 Warren, Rick, *The Purpose Driven Life: What on Earth Am I Here For?* (Zondervan, 2012)

everyday resources

BRANDS WE THINK GET IT RIGHT, AND DO IT WELL
AColdWall – @acoldwall
Labrum London – @labrumlondon
Food&Lycra – @foodandlycra
Wales Bonner – @walesbonner
Dizziak – @dizziaklondon
PAQ – @paq.works

INSIGHTFUL PODCASTS WE LOVE LISTENING TO
TRAINED by Nike
Honestly Podcast with Clemmie Telford
This City with Clara Amfo
About Race with Reni Eddo-Lodge
As Me with Sinéad
Exponential View by Azeem Azhar
Moonshot with Mike Parsons and Mark Pearson
Receipts Podcast with Tolani Shoneye, Milena
    Sanchez and Audrey Indome
Have You Heard George's Podcast? by George
    The Poet

INSIGHT RESOURCES WE LEARN WITH

Think With Google – www.thinkwithgoogle.com/
consumer-insights
Reddit – www.reddit.com/reddits
Mintel – www.store.mintel.com
YouGov – www.yougov.co.uk/topics

ORGANISATIONS THAT ARE CHANGING THE INDUSTRY

TheOtherBox – @_theotherbox
POCC – @wearepocc
Fearless Futures – @fearlessfutures
Creative Mentor Network – @creativementornetwork
Creative Access – @_creativeaccess

acknowledgements

To my parents and grandparents who taught me the meaning of hard work and the immigrant hustle. To my family, Tin and Neriah for being an endless source of inspiration, being patient and supportive through it all. To my mentors, colleagues, friends in the industry that opened doors, shared knowledge and collaborated with me over the last twelve years.

Niran,
2020

To my Dad, Mum and Nana for an unashamedly Nigerian upbringing, I'm proud of everything you have achieved. To Tolu and Moradeke for humbling and uplifting me from day one. To our partners who have tolerated us through this process, we appreciate you. To the friends and colleagues who have taught me valuable lessons. And a shout out to Yahweh for the continued opportunities.

Damola,
2020

NOTES

NOTES

NOTES

NOTES

UNLOCK YOUR POTENTIAL
WITH THE *HOW TO* SERIES
FROM

AVAILABLE NOW

FOLLOW @MERKYBOOKS FOR NEWS ON THE NEXT *HOW TO* RELEASES ...